Counting Money!

by M. W. Penn

Consulting Editor: Gail Saunders-Smith, PhD

CAPSTONE PRESS
a capstone imprint

Pebble Books are published by Capstone Press,
1710 Roe Crest Drive, North Mankato, MN 56003.
www.capstonepub.com

Books published by Capstone Press are manufactured with paper
containing at least 10 percent post-consumer waste.

Library of Congress Cataloging-in-Publication Data
Penn, M. W. (Marianne W.), 1944–
  Counting money! / by M. W. Penn.
    p. cm. — (Pebble books. Pebble math)
  Includes bibliographical references and index.
  Summary: "Simple rhyming text and color photographs describe counting
money"—Provided by publisher.
  ISBN 978-1-4296-7562-8 (library binding) — ISBN 978-1-4296-7875-9 (paperback)
  1. Counting—Juvenile literature. 2. Money—Juvenile literature. I. Title.
  QA113.P46 2012
  332.4'973—dc23   2011029946

Note to Parents and Teachers

The Pebble Math set supports national mathematics standards
related to algebra and geometry. This book describes and
illustrates counting money. The images support early readers in
understanding the text. The repetition of words and phrases helps
early readers learn new words. This book also introduces early
readers to subject-specific vocabulary words, which are defined
in the Glossary section. Early readers may need assistance to read
some words and to use the Table of Contents, Glossary, Read More,
Internet Sites, and Index sections of the book.

Printed in the United States of America in North Mankato, Minnesota.

102011   006405CGS12

Table of Contents

Let's Count! 5

What Is It Worth? 7

Counting Coins 15

Glossary 22

Read More 23

Internet Sites. 23

Index 24

Let's Count!

Some coins are worth a little.

Some coins are worth much more.

Let's learn the value of each coin

And count as we explore.

What Is It Worth?

A penny equals

Just 1 cent.

Count each penny

That you spent.

25¢
Just 5 nickels
for a pickle!

Original Fla
Banana
Birthday Ca
Black Cher
Blue Raspl
Bubblegum
Cantaloupe
Cherry
Coconut
Cola

Special R
Apple Pie A La
Banana Berry
Banana Colada
Banana Creme
Banana Split
Blue Hawaii
Cherry Bomb
Cherry Cola
Cherry Lime
Cherry Pie
Chocolate Coco
Chocolate Cover
Coconut Creme

SHAVE

FOOTLO
ICED CC
SODA &
MT. DEW, DIET M

WASECA
Sno

1 nickel is worth 5 cents.

Skip by fives to count.

5, 10, 15, 20:

What's the next amount?

10¢ a glass

1 dime equals 10 cents,

Although the coin is small.

Counting dimes is easy.

Skip count by 10 for all.

It's the biggest! That makes sense!

1 quarter equals 25 cents.

1 quarter is worth 5 nickels, true.

And 2 dimes plus 1 nickel too.

Counting Coins

1 nickel equals 5 pennies.

2 nickels equal 1 dime.

5 nickels equal 1 quarter.

Learn this nickel rhyme.

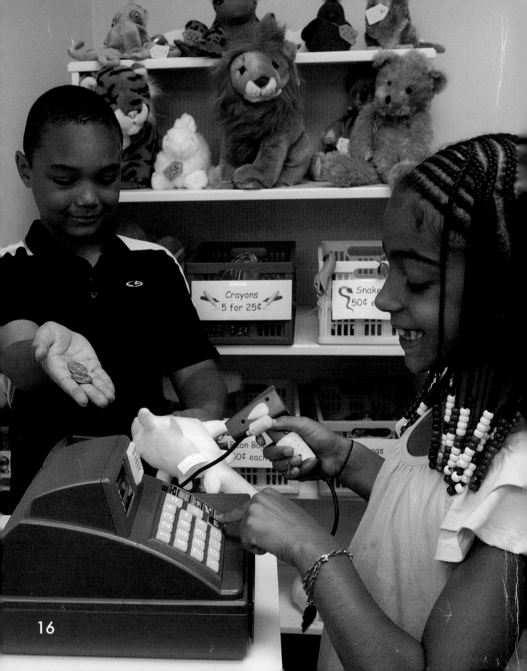

Crayons
5 for 25¢

Snake
50¢ e

25¢

an B
0¢ eac

16

10 nickels are worth 50 cents.

5 dimes are worth the same.

2 quarters equal 50 cents.

Play this counting game.

Here's a counting game that's great!

Which coins add up to 48?

4 dimes, 8 pennies. Nothing to it!

Find other groups of coins that do it.

penny

nickel

dime

quarter

Know the value of each coin.

Place the coins in order:

Penny, nickel, slender dime

And the big round quarter.

Glossary

add—to find the sum of two or more numbers

equal—the same as; an equal sign is shown as =

plus—to add something; a plus sign is shown as +

skip count—to count by skipping 1 or more numbers according to a pattern; skip counting is often done by 2s or 5s

value—how much something is worth

Read More

Kompelien, Tracy. *I Know about Money, It's So Funny!* Math Made Fun. Edina, Minn.: Abdo Pub. Co., 2007.

Marks, Jennifer L. *Sorting Money.* Sorting. Mankato, Minn.: Capstone Press, 2007.

Wingard-Nelson, Rebecca. *I Can Count Money.* I Like Money Math! Berkeley Heights, N.J.: Enslow Elementary, 2009.

Internet Sites

FactHound offers a safe, fun way to find Internet sites related to this book. All of the sites on FactHound have been researched by our staff.

Here's all you do:

Visit *www.facthound.com*

Type in this code: 9781429675628

Super-cool stuff!

Check out projects, games and lots more at
www.capstonekids.com

Index

biggest coin, 13

dimes, 11, 13, 15, 17,
   19, 21

nickels, 9, 13, 15, 17, 21

pennies, 7, 15, 19, 21

quarters, 13, 15, 17, 21

skip counting, 9, 11

value, 5, 21

Word Count: 187
Grade: 1
Early-Intervention Level: 14

Editorial Credits
Gillia Olson, editor; Bobbie Nuytten, designer; Sarah Schuette, photo stylist;
   Marcy Morin, studio scheduler; Kathy McColley, production specialist

Photo Credits
All photos by Capstone Studio: Karon Dubke

The author dedicates this book to Michael Siuta and the Ten County Mathematics
Educators Association (New York).